LOVE YOUR MASS

APOSTOLIC LETTER
OF THE SUPREME PONTIFF
JOHN PAUL II
ON THE 25TH ANNIVERSARY
OF THE PROMULGATION
OF THE CONCILIAR CONSTITUTION
SACROSANCTUM CONCILIUM
ON THE SACRED LITURGY

CATHOLIC TRUTH SOCIETY

PUBLISHERS TO THE HOLY SEE
LONDON

First published 1989 by the
Incorporated Catholic Truth Society
38–40 Eccleston Square
London SW1V 1PD

ISBN 0 85183 785 9

Printed by The Ludo Press Ltd, London SW18 3DG

To all my Brothers
in the Episcopate and the Priesthood
Greetings and the Apostolic Blessing

1. TWENTY-FIVE YEARS ago on 4th December 1963 the Supreme Pontiff Paul VI promulgated the Constitution *Sacrosanctum Concilium* on the Sacred Liturgy, which the Fathers of the Second Vatican Council, gathered in the Holy Spirit, had approved but a short time before.[1] It was a memorable event on several accounts. Indeed, it was the first fruit of the Council, called by Pope John XXIII, to update the Church. The moment had been prepared for by a great liturgical and pastoral movement, and was a source of hope for the life and the renewal of the Church.

In putting into practice the reform of the Liturgy, the Council achieved in a special way the fundamental aim which it had set itself: "To impart an ever increasing vigour to the Christian life of the faithful; to adapt more suitably to the needs of our own times those

[1] AAS 56 (1964), pp. 97-134.

institutions that are subject to change; to foster whatever can promote union among all who believe in Christ; to strengthen whatever can help to call the whole of humanity into the household of the Church".[2]

2. From the beginning of my pastoral ministry in the See of Peter, I have taken care "to state the lasting importance of the Second Vatican Council", calling attention to "our clear duty to devote our energies to putting it into effect". Our efforts have been directed towards "bringing to maturity in the sense of movement and of life the fruitful seeds which the Fathers of the Ecumenical Council, nourished with the word of God, cast upon the good soil (cf. *Mt* 13:8, 23), that is, their authoritative teaching and pastoral decisions".[3] On several occasions I have developed various aspects of the conciliar teaching on the Liturgy,[4] and have emphasized the importance of the Constitution *Sacrosanctum Concilium* for the life of the people of God: in it

[2] Second Vatican Council, Constitution on the Sacred Liturgy *Sacrosanctum Concilium*, 1.

[3] First message to the world (17 October 1978): *AAS* 70 (1978), pp. 920-921.

[4] Cf. especially: Encyclical Letter *Redemptor Hominis* (4 March 1979), 7. 18-22: *AAS* 71 (1979) 23. 27-30. 33. 37. 48. 53-55. 66-68, pp. 1296-1297, 1298-1303, 1305-1306, 1308-1309, 1316: Letter *Dominicae Cenae*, On the mystery and worship of the Holy Eucharist (24 February 1980); *AAS* 72 (1980), pp. 113-148; Encyclical Letter *Dives in Misericordia* (30 November 1980), 13-15: *AAS* 72 (1980), pp. 1218-1232: Apostolic Exhortation *Familiaris Consortio* (22 November 1981), 13. 15. 19-21. 33. 38-39. 55-59. 66-68: *AAS* (1982), pp. 93-96, 97, 101-106, 120-123, 129-131, 147-152, 159-165; Post-Synodal Apostolic Exhortation *Reconciliatio et Paenitentia* (2 December 1984): *AAS* 77 (1985), pp. 185-275, especially nos. 23-33, pp. 233-271.

"the substance of that ecclesiological doctrine which would later be put before the conciliar Assembly is already evident. The Constitution *Sacrosanctum Concilium*, the first conciliar document, anticipated"[5] the Dogmatic Constitution *Lumen Gentium* on the Church and amplified, in its turn, the teaching of the Constitution.

After a quarter of a century, during which both Church and society have experienced profound and rapid changes, it is a fitting moment to throw light on the importance of the Conciliar Constitution, its relevance in relation to new problems and the enduring value of its principles.

[5] Address to the Congress of Presidents and Secretaries of National Liturgical Commissions (27 October 1984), 1: *Insegnamenti*, VII, 2 (1984), p. 1049.

I
RENEWAL IN ACCORD WITH TRADITION

3. In response to the requests of the Fathers of the Council of Trent, concerned with the reform of the Church in their time, Pope Saint Pius V saw to the reform of the liturgical books, above all the Breviary and the Missal. It was towards this same goal that the succeeding Roman Pontiffs directed their energies during the subsequent centuries in order to ensure that the rites and liturgical books were brought up to date and when necessary clarified. From the beginning of this century they undertook a more general reform.

Pope Saint Pius X established a special Commission for this reform, and he thought that it would take a number of years for it to complete its work; however, he laid the foundation stone of this edifice by renewing the celebration of Sunday and by reforming the Roman Breviary.[6] "In fact this all demands", he affirmed, "according to the views of the experts, a work

[6] Apostolic Constitution *Divino Afflatu* (1 November 1911): *AAS* 3 (1911), pp. 633-638.

both detailed and extensive; and therefore it is necessary that many years should pass, before this liturgical *edifice,* so to speak, ... reappears in new splendour in its dignity and harmony, once the marks of old age have been cleared away".[7]

Pope Pius XII took up again the great project of liturgical reform by issuing the Encyclical *Mediator Dei*[8] and by establishing a new Commission.[9] He likewise decided important matters, for example: authorizing a new version of the Psalter to facilitate the understanding of the Psalms;[10] the modification of the Eucharistic fast in order to facilitate access to Holy Communion; the use of contemporary language in the Ritual; and, above all, the reform of the Easter Vigil[11] and Holy Week.[12]

The introduction to the *Roman Missal* of 1963 was preceded by the declaration of Pope John XXIII, according to which "the fundamental principles, related to the general reform of the Liturgy, were to be entrusted to the Fathers in the forthcoming Ecumenical Council".[13]

[7] Motu Proprio *Abbinc Duos Annos* (23 October 1913): *AAS* 5 (1913), pp. 449-450.

[8] 20 November 1947: *AAS* 39 (1947), pp. 521-600.

[9] Sacred Congregation of Rites, Historical Section No. 71, *Memoria sulla riforma liturgica* (1946).

[10] Pius XII, Motu Proprio *In Cotidianis Precibus* (24 March 1945): *AAS* 37 (1945), pp. 65-67.

[11] Sacred Congregation of Rites, Decree *Dominicae Resurrectionis* (9 February 1951): *AAS* 43 (1951), pp. 128-129.

[12] Sacred Congregation of Rites, Decree *Maxima Redemptionis* (16 November 1955): *AAS* 47 (1955), pp. 838-841.

[13] John XXIII, Apostolic Letter *Rubricarum Instructum* (25 July 1960): *AAS* 52 (1960), p. 594.

4. Such an overall reform of the Liturgy was in harmony with the general hope of the whole Church. In fact, the liturgical spirit had become more and more widespread together with the desire for an "active participation in the most holy mysteries and in the public and solemn prayer of the Church",[14] and a wish to hear the word of God in more abundant measure. Together with the biblical renewal, the ecumenical movement, the missionary impetus and ecclesiological research, the reform of the Liturgy was to contribute to the overall renewal of the Church. I drew attention to this in the Letter *Dominicae Cenae:* "A very close and organic *bond exists between the renewal of the Liturgy and the renewal of the whole life of the Church*. The Church not only acts but also expresses herself in the Liturgy and draws from the Liturgy the strength for her life".[15]

The reform of the rites and the liturgical books was undertaken immediately after the promulgation of the Constitution *Sacrosanctum Concilium* and was brought to an effective conclusion in a few years thanks to the considerable and selfless work of a large number of experts and Bishops from all parts of the world.[16]

This work was undertaken in accordance

[14] Pius X, Motu Proprio *Tra le sollecitudini dell'officio pastorale* (22 November 1903): *Pii X Pontificis Maximi Acta,* 1, p. 77.

[15] Letter *Dominicae Cenae* (24 February 1980), 13; *AAS* 72 (1980), p. 146.

[16] Cf. Second Vatican Council, Constitution on the Sacred Liturgy *Sacrosanctum Concilium*, 25.

with the conciliar principles of fidelity to tradition and openness to legitimate development,[17] and so it is possible to say that the reform of the Liturgy is strictly traditional and in accordance with "the ancient usage of the holy Fathers".[18]

[17] Cf. *ibid.* 23.
[18] Cf. *ibid,* 50; Roman Missal, Preface, 6.

II
THE GUIDING PRINCIPLES OF THE CONSTITUTION

5. The guiding principles of the Constitution, which were the basis of the reform, remain fundamental in the task of leading the faithful to an active celebration of the mysteries, "the primary and indispensable source of the true Christian spirit".[19] Now that the greater part of the liturgical books have been published, translated and brought into use, it is still necessary to keep these principles constantly in mind and to build upon them.

a) The Re-enactment of the Paschal Mystery

6. The first principle is the re-enactment of the Paschal Mystery of Christ in the Liturgy of the Church, based on the fact that "it was from the side of Christ as he slept upon the Cross that there issued forth the sublime sacrament of the

[19] Second Vatican Council, Constitution on the Sacred Liturgy *Sacrosanctum Concilium*, 14.

whole Church".[20] The whole of liturgical life gravitates about the Eucharistic Sacrifice and the other sacraments, in which we draw upon the living springs of salvation (cf. *Is* 12:3).[21]

Hence we must have a sufficient awareness that through the "Paschal Mystery we have been buried with Christ in Baptism, so that we may rise with him to a new life".[22] When the faithful participate in the Eucharist, they must understand that truly "each time we offer this memorial sacrifice the work of our redemption is accomplished",[23] and to this end Bishops must carefully train the faithful to celebrate every Sunday the marvellous work that Christ has wrought in the mystery of his Passover, in order that they likewise may proclaim it to the world.[24] In the hearts of all, Bishops and faithful, Easter must regain its unique importance in the liturgical year, so that it really is the Feast of Feasts.

Since Christ's Death on the Cross and his Resurrection constitute the content of the daily life of the Church[25] and the pledge of his eternal

[20] Second Vatican Council, Constitution on the Sacred Liturgy *Sacrosanctum Concilium,* 5; Roman Missal, The Easter Vigil: Prayer after the 7th Reading.

[21] Second Vatican Council, Constitution on the Sacred Liturgy *Sacrosanctum Concilium,* 5-6. 47. 61. 102. 106-107.

[22] Roman Missal, The Easter Vigil, Renewal of Baptismal Promises.

[23] *Ibid.,* Evening Mass " In Cena Domini ", Prayer over the Gifts.

[24] Cf. *ibid.,* Preface of Sundays in Ordinary Time, 1.

[25] Cf. Encyclical Letter *Redemptor Hominis* (4 March 1979), 7: *AAS* 71 (1979), pp. 268-270.

Passover,[26] the Liturgy has as its first task to lead us untiringly back to the Easter pilgrimage initiated by Christ, in which we accept death in order to enter into life.

7. In order to re-enact his Paschal Mystery, Christ is ever present in his Church, especially in liturgical celebrations.[27] Hence the Liturgy is the privileged place for the encounter of Christians with God and the one whom he has sent, Jesus Christ (cf. *Jn* 17:3).

Christ is present in the Church assembled at prayer in his name. It is this fact which gives such a unique character to the Christian assembly with the consequent duties not only of brotherly welcome but also of forgiveness (cf. *Mt* 5:23-24), and of dignity in behaviour, gesture and song.

Christ is present and acts in the person of the ordained minister who celebrates.[28] The priest is not merely entrusted with a function, but in virtue of the Ordination received he has been consecrated to act "*in persona Christi*". To this consecration there must be a corresponding disposition, both inward and outward, also reflected in liturgical vestments, in the place which he occupies and in the word which he utters.

[26] Cf. Letter *Dominicae Cenae* (24 February 1980), 4; *AAS* 72 (1980), p. 119-121.

[27] Cf. Second Vatican Council, Constitution on the Sacred Liturgy *Sacrosanctum Concilium,* 7; cf. Paul VI, Encyclical Letter *Mysterium Fidei* (3 September 1965); *AAS* 57 (1965), pp. 762. 764.

[28] Cf. Sacred Congregation of Rites, Instruction *Eucharisticum Mysterium* (25 May 1967), 9: *AAS* 59 (1967), p. 547.

Christ is present in his word as proclaimed in the assembly and which, commented upon in the homily, is to be listened to in faith and assimilated in prayer. All this must derive from the dignity of the book and of the place appointed for the proclamation of the word of God, and from the attitude of the reader, based upon an awareness of the fact that the reader is the spokesman of God before his or her brothers and sisters.

Christ is present and acts by the power of the Holy Spirit in the sacraments and, in a special and pre-eminent fashion (*sublimiori modo*), in the Sacrifice of the Mass under the Eucharistic Species,[29] also when these are reserved in the tabernacle apart from the celebration with a view to Communion of the sick and adoration by the faithful.[30] With regard to this real and mysterious presence, it is the duty of pastors to recall frequently in their catechetical instructions the teaching of the faith, a teaching that the faithful must live out and that theologians are called upon to expound. Faith in this presence of the Lord involves an outward sign of respect towards the church, the holy place in which God manifests himself in mystery (cf. *Ex* 3:5), especially during the celebration of the sacraments: holy things must always be treated in a holy manner.

[29] Cf. Paul VI, Encyclical Letter *Mysterium Fidei* (3 September 1965): *AAS* 57 (1965), p. 763.
[30] Cf. *ibid.*, pp. 769-771.

b) THE READING OF THE WORD OF GOD

8. The second principle is the presence of the word of God.

The Constitution *Sacrosanctum Concilium* sets out likewise to restore a "more abundant reading from Holy Scripture, one more varied and more appropriate".[31] The basic reason for this restoration is expressed both in the Constitution on the Liturgy, namely, so that "the intimate link between rite and word" may be manifested,[32] and also in the Dogmatic Constitution on Divine Revelation, which teaches: "The Church has always venerated the divine Scriptures, just as she has venerated the very body of the Lord, never ceasing above all in the Sacred Liturgy to nourish herself on the bread of life at the table both of the word of God, and of the Body of Christ, and to minister it to the faithful".[33] Growth in liturgical life and consequently progress in Christian life cannot be achieved except by continually promoting among the faithful, and above all among priests, a "warm and living knowledge of Scripture".[34] The word of God is now better known in the Christian communities, but a true renewal sets further and ever new requirements: fidelity to the authentic

[31] Second Vatican Council, Constitution on the Sacred Liturgy *Sacrosanctum Concilium*, 35.

[32] *Ibid.*

[33] Second Vatican Council, Constitution on the Divine Revelation *Dei Verbum*, 21.

[34] Second Vatican Council, Constitution on the Sacred Liturgy *Sacrosanctum Concilium*, 24.

meaning of the Scriptures which must never be lost from view, especially when the Scriptures are translated into different languages; the manner of proclaiming the word of God so that it may be perceived for what it is; the use of appropriate technical means, the interior disposition of the ministers of the word so that they carry out properly their function in the liturgical assembly;[35] careful preparation of the homily through study and meditation; effort on the part of the faithful to participate at the table of the word; a taste for prayer with the Psalms; a desire to discover Christ — like the disciples at Emmaus — at the table of the word and the bread.[36]

c) THE SELF-MANIFESTATION OF THE CHURCH

9. Finally, the Council saw in the Liturgy an epiphany of the Church: it is the Church at prayer. In celebrating Divine Worship the Church gives expression to what she is: One, Holy, Catholic and Apostolic.

The Church manifests herself as *one*, with that unity which comes to her from the Trinity,[37] especially when the holy people of God partici-

[35] Cf. Letter *Dominicae Cenae* (24 February 1980), 10: *AAS* 72 (1980), pp. 134-137.

[36] Cf. Liturgy of the Hours, Monday of Week IV, Prayer at Evening Prayer.

[37] Cf. Roman Missal, Preface of Sundays in Ordinary Time, VIII.

pates "in the one Eucharist, in one and the same prayer, at the one altar, presided over by the Bishop surrounded by his presbyterate and his ministers".[38] Let nothing disrupt or obscure in the celebration of the Liturgy this unity of the Church!

The Church expresses the *holiness* that comes to her from Christ (cf. *Eph* 5:26-27) when, gathered in one body by the Holy Spirit[39] who makes holy and gives life,[40] she communicates to the faithful by means of the Eucharist and the other sacraments all the graces and blessings of the Father.[41]

In liturgical celebration the Church expresses her *catholicity*, since the Spirit of the Lord gathers together in her people of all languages in the profession of the same faith[42] and from East and West presents to God the Father the offering of Christ, and offers herself together with him.[43]

In the Liturgy the Church manifests herself as *apostolic*, because the faith that she professes is founded upon the witness of the Apostles; because in the celebration of the Mysteries, presided over by the Bishop, successor of the Apostles, or by a minister ordained in the Apostolic

[38] Second Vatican Council, Constitution on the Sacred Liturgy *Sacrosanctum Concilium*, 41.

[39] Cf. *Roman Missal,* Eucharistic Prayers II and IV.

[40] Cf. *ibid.,* Eucharistic Prayer III; Nicene-Constantinopolitan Creed.

[41] Cf. *ibid.,* Eucharistic Prayer I.

[42] Cf. *ibid.,* Solemn Blessing on Pentecost Sunday.

[43] Cf. *ibid.,* Eucharistic Prayer III.

succession, she faithfully hands on what she has received from the Apostolic Tradition; and because the worship which she renders to God commits her to the mission of spreading the Gospel in the world.

Thus it is especially in the Liturgy that the Mystery of the Church is proclaimed, experienced and lived.[44]

[44] Cf. Address to the Congress of Presidents and Secretaries of National Liturgical Commissions (27 October 1984), 1: *Insegnamenti,* VII 2 (1984), p. 1049.

III
GUIDELINES FOR THE RENEWAL OF LITURGICAL LIFE

10. From these principles are derived certain norms and guidelines which must govern the renewal of liturgical life. While the reform of the Liturgy desired by the Second Vatican Council can be considered already in progress, the pastoral promotion of the Liturgy constitutes a permanent commitment to draw ever more abundantly from the riches of the Liturgy that vital force which spreads from Christ to the members of his Body which is the Church.

Since the Liturgy is the exercise of the priesthood of Christ, it is necessary to keep ever alive the affirmation of the disciple faced with the mysterious presence of Christ: "It is the Lord!" (*Jn* 21:7). Nothing of what we do in the Liturgy can appear more important than what in an unseen but real manner Christ accomplishes by the power of his Spirit. A faith alive in charity, adoration, praise of the Father and silent contemplation will always be the prime objective of liturgical and sacramental pastoral care.

Since the Liturgy is totally permeated by the word of God, any other word must be in harmony with it, above all in the homily but also in the various interventions of the minister and in the hymns which are sung. No other reading may supplant the Biblical word, and the words of men must be at the service of the word of God without obscuring it.

Since liturgical celebrations are not private acts but "celebrations of the Church, the 'sacrament of unity'",[45] their regulation is dependent solely upon the hierarchical authority of the Church.[46] The Liturgy belongs to the whole body of the Church.[47] It is for this reason that it is not permitted to anyone, even the priest, or any group, to add, subtract or change anything whatsoever on their own initiative.[48] Fidelity to the rites and to the authentic texts of the Liturgy is a requirement of the *Lex orandi*, which must always be in conformity with the *Lex credendi*. A lack of fidelity on this point may even affect the very validity of the sacraments.

Since it is a celebration of the Church, the Liturgy requires the active, conscious and full participation of all, according to the diversity of Orders and of office.[49] All, the ministers and the other faithful, in the accomplishment of their

[45] Second Vatican Council, Constitution on the Sacred Liturgy *Sacrosanctum Concilium*, 26.

[46] Cf. *ibid.*, 22 and 26.

[47] Cf. *ibid.*, 26.

[48] Cf. *ibid.*, 22.

[49] Cf. *ibid.*, 26.

particular function, do that and only that which is proper to them.[50] It is for this reason that the Church gives preference to celebrations in common, when the nature of the rites implies this;[51] she encourages the formation of ministers, readers, cantors and commentators, who carry out a true liturgical ministry;[52] she has restored concelebration,[53] and she recommends the common celebration of the Liturgy of the Hours.[54]

Given that the Liturgy is the school of the prayer of the Church, it has been considered good to introduce and develop the use of the vernacular—without diminishing the use of Latin, retained by the Council for the Latin Rite[55]—so that every individual can understand and proclaim in his or her mother tongue the wonders of God (cf. *Acts* 2:11). It has likewise been considered good to increase the number of Prefaces and Eucharistic Prayers, so as to enrich the Church's treasury of prayer and an understanding of the mystery of Christ.

Since the Liturgy has great pastoral value, the liturgical books have provided for a certain degree of adaptation to the assembly and to individuals, with the possibility of openness to

[50] Cf. *ibid.*, 28.

[51] Cf. *ibid.*, 27.

[52] Cf. *ibid.*, 29.

[53] Cf. *ibid.*, 57; cf. Sacred Congregation of Rites, General Decree *Ecclesiae Semper* (7 March 1965): *AAS* 57 (1965), pp. 410-412.

[54] Second Vatican Council, Constitution on the Sacred Liturgy *Sacrosanctum Concilium*, 99.

[55] Cf. *ibid.*, 36.

the traditions and culture of different peoples.[56] The revision of the rites has sought a noble simplicity[57] and signs that are easily understood, but the desired simplicity must not degenerate into an impoverishment of the signs. On the contrary, the signs, above all the sacramental signs, must be easily grasped but carry the greatest possible expressiveness. Bread and wine, water and oil, and also incense, ashes, fire and flowers, and indeed almost all the elements of creation have their place in the Liturgy as gifts to the Creator and as a contribution to the dignity and beauty of the celebration.

[56] Cf. *ibid.*, 37-40.
[57] Cf. *ibid.*, 34.

IV
THE PRACTICAL APPLICATION OF THE REFORM

a) Difficulties

11. It must be recognized that the application of the liturgical reform has met with difficulties due especially to an unfavourable environment marked by a tendency to see religious practice as something of a private affair, by a certain rejection of institutions, by a decrease in the visibility of the Church in society, and by a calling into question of personal faith. It can also be supposed that the transition from simply being present, very often in a rather passive and silent way, to a fuller and more active participation has been for some people too demanding. Different and even contradictory reactions to the reform have resulted from this. Some have received the new books with a certain indifference, or without trying to understand or help others to understand the reasons for the changes; others, unfortunately, have turned back in a one-sided and exclusive way to the previous liturgical forms which some of them consider to be the sole guarantee of certainty in

faith. Others have promoted outlandish innovations, departing from the norms issued by the authority of the Apostolic See or the Bishops, thus disrupting the unity of the Church and the piety of the faithful, and even on occasion contradicting matters of faith.

b) Positive results

12. This should not lead anyone to forget that the vast majority of the pastors and the Christian people have accepted the liturgical reform in a spirit of obedience and indeed joyful fervour.

For this we should give thanks to God for that movement of the Holy Spirit in the Church which the liturgical renewal represents; [58] for the fact that the table of the word of God is now abundantly furnished for all; [59] for the immense effort undertaken throughout the world to provide the Christian people with translations of the Bible, the Missal and other liturgical books; for the increased participation of the faithful by prayer and song, gesture and silence, in the Eucharist and the other sacraments; for the ministries exercised by lay people and the responsibilities that they have assumed in virtue of the

[58] Cf. *ibid.*, 43.

[59] Cf. Second Vatican Council, Dogmatic Constitution on Divine Revelation *Dei Verbum*, 21; Constitution *Sacrosanctum Concilium*, 51.

common priesthood into which they have been initiated through Baptism and Confirmation; for the radiant vitality of so many Christian communities, a vitality drawn from the well-spring of the Liturgy.

These are all reasons for holding fast to the teaching of the Constitution *Sacrosanctum Concilium* and to the reforms which it has made possible: "the liturgical renewal is the most visible fruit of the whole work of the Council".[60] For many people the message of the Second Vatican Council has been experienced principally through the liturgical reform.

c) Erroneous applications

13. Side by side with these benefits of the liturgical reform, one has to acknowledge with regret deviations of greater or lesser seriousness in its application.

On occasion there have been noted illicit omissions or additions, rites invented outside the framework of established norms; postures or songs which are not conducive to faith or to a sense of the sacred; abuses in the practice of general absolution; confusion between the ministerial priesthood, linked with Ordination, and the common priesthood of the faithful, which has its foundation in Baptism.

[60] *Final Report of the Extraordinary Assembly of the Synod of Bishops* (7 December 1985), II, B, b, 1.

It cannot be tolerated that certain priests should take upon themselves the right to compose Eucharistic Prayers or to substitute profane readings for texts from Sacred Scripture. Initiatives of this sort, far from being linked with the liturgical reform as such, or with the books which have issued from it, are in direct contradiction to it, disfigure it and deprive the Christian people of the genuine treasures of the Liturgy of the Church.

It is for the Bishops to root out such abuses, because the regulation of the Liturgy depends on the Bishop within the limits of the law [61] and because "the life in Christ of his faithful people in some sense is derived from and depends upon him".[62]

[61] Second Vatican Council, Constitution on the Sacred Liturgy *Sacrosanctum Concilium*, 22, 1.

[62] *Ibid.*, 41.

V
THE FUTURE OF THE RENEWAL

14. The Constitution *Sacrosanctum Concilium* is the expression of the unanimous voice of the College of Bishops gathered around the Successor of Peter and with the help of the Spirit of Truth promised by the Lord Jesus (cf. *Jn* 15:26). The Constitution continues to sustain the Church along the paths of renewal and of holiness by fostering genuine liturgical life.

The principles enunciated in that document are an orientation also for the future of the Liturgy, in such a way that the liturgical reform may be ever better understood and implemented. "It is therefore necessary and urgent to actuate a new and *intensive education* in order to discover all the richness contained in the Liturgy".[63]

The Liturgy of the Church goes beyond the liturgical reform. We are not in the same situation as obtained in 1963: a generation of priests and of faithful which has not known the liturgical books prior to the reform now acts with responsibility in the Church and society. One can-

[63] Letter *Dominicae Cenae*, (24 February 1980), *AAS* 72 (1980), p. 133.

not therefore continue to speak of change as it was spoken of at the time of the Constitution's publication; rather one has to speak of an ever deeper grasp of the Liturgy of the Church, celebrated according to the current books and lived above all as a reality in the spiritual order.

a) Biblical and Liturgical Formation

15. The most urgent task is that of the biblical and liturgical formation of the people of God, both pastors and faithful. The Constitution had already stressed this: "there is no hope that this may come to pass unless pastors of souls themselves become imbued more deeply with the spirit and power of the Liturgy so as to become masters of it".[64] This is a long-term programme, which must begin in the Seminaries and Houses of Formation[65] and continue throughout their priestly life.[66] A formation suited to their state is indispensable also for lay people,[67] especially since in many regions they are

[64] Second Vatican Council, Constitution on the Sacred Liturgy *Sacrosanctum Concilium,* 14.

[65] Cf. Sacred Congregation of Rites, Instruction *Inter Oecumenici* (26 September 1964), 11-13: *AAS* 56 (1964), pp. 879-880; Sacred Congregation for Catholic Education, *Ratio Fundamentalis* on priestly formation (6 January 1970), cap. VIII: *AAS* 62 (1970), pp. 351-361; Instruction *In Ecclesiasticam Futurorum,* On Liturgical formation in Seminaries (3 June 1979), Rome 1979.

[66] Cf. Sacred Congregation of Rites, Instruction *Inter Oecumenici* (26 September 1964), 14-17: *AAS* 56 (1964) pp. 880-881.

[67] Second Vatican Council, Constitution on the Sacred Liturgy *Sacrosanctum Concilium,* 19.

called upon to assume ever more important responsibilities in the community.

b) Adaptation

16. Another important task for the future is that of the adaptation of the Liturgy to different cultures. The Constitution set forth the principle, indicating the procedure to be followed by the Episcopal Conferences.[68] The adaptation of languages has been rapidly accomplished, even if on occasion with some difficulties. It has been followed by the adaptation of rites, which is a more delicate matter but equally necessary. There remains the considerable task of continuing to implant the Liturgy in certain cultures, welcoming from them those expressions which are compatible with aspects of *the true and authentic spirit of the Liturgy,* in respect for the *substantial unity of the Roman Rite* as expressed in the liturgical books.[69] The adaptation must take account of the fact that in the Liturgy, and notably that of the sacraments, there is a *part which is unchangeable,* because it is of divine institution, and of which the Church is the guardian. There are also *parts open to change,* which the Church has the power and on occasion also the duty to adapt to the cultures of recently evangelized peoples.[70] This is not a new problem for the

[68] Cf. *ibid.*, 39.
[69] Cf. *ibid.*, 37-40.
[70] Cf. *ibid.*, 21.

Church. Liturgical diversity can be a source of enrichment, but it can also provoke tensions, mutual misunderstandings and even divisions. In this field it is clear that diversity must not damage unity. It can only gain expression in fidelity to the common Faith, to the sacramental signs that the Church has received from Christ and to hierarchical communion. Cultural adaptation also requires conversion of heart and even, where necessary, a breaking with ancestral customs incompatible with the Catholic faith. This demands a serious formation in theology, history and culture, as well as sound judgement in discerning what is necessary or useful and what is not useful or even dangerous to faith. "A satisfactory development in this area cannot but be the fruit of a progressive maturing in faith, one which encompasses spiritual discernment, theological lucidity, and a sense of the universal Church, acting in broad harmony".[71]

c) ATTENTION TO NEW PROBLEMS

17. The effort towards liturgical renewal must furthermore respond to the needs of our time. The Liturgy is not disincarnate.[72] In these twenty-five years new problems have arisen or

[71] Address to a group of Bishops from the Episcopal Conference of Zaire (12 April 1983), 5: *AAS* 75 (1983), p. 620.

[72] Cf. Address to the Congress of Presidents and Secretaries of National Liturgical Commissions (27 October 1984), 2: *Insegnamenti*, VII/2 (1984), p. 1051.

have assumed new importance, for example: the exercise of a diaconate open to married men; liturgical tasks in celebrations which can be entrusted to lay people; liturgical celebrations for children, for young people and the handicapped; the procedures for the composition of liturgical texts appropriate to a particular country.

In the Constitution *Sacrosanctum Concilium* there is no reference to these problems, but the general principles are given which serve to coordinate and promote liturgical life.

d) LITURGY AND POPULAR DEVOTIONS

18. Finally, to safeguard the reform and ensure the promotion of the Liturgy[73] it is necessary to take account of popular Christian devotion and its relation to liturgical life.[74] This popular devotion should not be ignored or treated with indifference or contempt, since it is rich in values,[75] and per se gives expression to the religious attitude towards God. But it needs to be continually evangelized, so that the faith which it expresses may become an ever more mature and authentic act. Both the pious exer-

[73] Cf. Second Vatican Council, Constitution on the Sacred Liturgy *Sacrosanctum Concilium,* 1.

[74] Cf. *ibid.,* 12-13.

[75] Cf. Paul VI, Apostolic Exhortation *Evangelii Nuntiandi* (8 December 1975), 48: *AAS* 68 (1976), pp. 37-38.

cises of the Christian people[76] and also other forms of devotion are welcomed and encouraged provided that they do not replace or intrude into liturgical celebrations. An authentic pastoral promotion of the Liturgy will build upon the riches of popular piety, purifying and directing them towards the Liturgy as the offering of the peoples.[77]

[76] Cf. Second Vatican Council, Constitution on the Sacred Liturgy *Sacrosanctum Concilium,* 13.

[77] Cf. Address to the Episcopal Conference of Abruzzo and Molise on *ad Limina* visit (24 April 1986), 3-7: *AAS* 78 (1986), pp. 1140-1143.

VI
THE ORGANISMS RESPONSIBLE FOR LITURGICAL RENEWAL

a) The Congregation for Divine Worship and the Discipline of the Sacraments

19. The task of promoting the renewal of the Liturgy pertains in the first place to the Apostolic See.[78] It was four hundred years ago that Pope Sixtus V created the Sacred Congregation of Rites and entrusted it with responsibility for keeping watch over the exercise of Divine Worship, reformed after the Council of Trent. Pope Saint Pius X instituted another Congregation for the Discipline of the Sacraments. With a view to the practical implementation of the Second Vatican Council's Constitution on the Liturgy, Pope Paul VI instituted a *Consilium*,[79] later the Sacred Congregation for Divine Worship,[80] and they carried out the task entrusted to them with generosity, competence and promptness.

[78] Cf. Second Vatican Council, Constitution on the Sacred Liturgy *Sacrosanctum Concilium*, 22, 1.

[79] Apostolic Letter *Sacram Liturgiam* (25 January 1964): *AAS* 56 (1964), pp. 139-144.

[80] Apostolic Constitution *Sacra Rituum Congregatio* (8 May 1969): *AAS* 61 (1969), pp. 297-305.

In accordance with the new structure of the Roman Curia as laid down by the Apostolic Constitution *Pastor Bonus,* the whole area of Sacred Liturgy is brought together and placed under the responsibility of a single Dicastery: the Congregation for Divine Worship and the Discipline of the Sacraments. Always taking into account the area of competence of the Congregation for the Doctrine of the Faith,[81] it pertains to this Congregation to regulate and promote the Liturgy, of which the Sacraments are the essential part, by encouraging pastoral liturgical activities,[82] supporting the various Organisms devoted to the liturgical apostolate, music, song and sacred art,[83] and keeping watch over sacramental discipline.[84] This is a work of importance, for it concerns above all the faithful preservation of the great principles of the Catholic Liturgy, as illustrated and developed in the Conciliar Constitution. It is likewise a question of drawing upon these principles for inspiration in promoting and deepening throughout the Church the renewal of liturgical life.

The Congregation will assist Diocesan Bishops in their efforts to offer to God true Christian worship and to regulate it according to the precepts of the Lord and the laws of the

[81] Apostolic Constitution *Pastor Bonus* (28 June 1988), 62: *AAS* 80 (1988), p. 876.
[82] Cf. *ibid.,* 64: *l.c.,* pp. 876-877.
[83] Cf. *ibid.,* 65: *l.c.,* pp. 877.
[84] Cf. *ibid.,* 63 and 66: *l.c.,* pp. 876 and 877.

Church.[85] It will be in close and trusting contact with the Episcopal Conferences for all that pertains to their competence in the liturgical field.[86]

b) The Episcopal Conferences

20. The Episcopal Conferences have had the weighty responsibility of preparing the translations of the liturgical books.[87] Immediate need occasionally led to the use of provisional translations, approved *ad interim*. But now the time has come to reflect upon certain difficulties that have subsequently emerged, to remedy certain defects or inaccuracies, to complete partial translations, to compose or approve chants to be used in the Liturgy, to ensure respect for the texts approved and lastly to publish liturgical books in a form that both testifies to the stability achieved and is worthy of the mysteries being celebrated.

For the work of translation, as well as for the wider implications of liturgical renewal for whole countries, each Episcopal Conference was required to establish a National Commission and ensure the collaboration of experts in the various sectors of liturgical science and

[85] Cf. Dogmatic Constitution on the Church *Lumen Gentium*, 26; Second Vatican Council, Constitution on the Sacred Liturgy *Sacrosanctum Concilium*, 22, 1.

[86] Cf. Apostolic Constitution *Pastor Bonus*, 64, 3: *l.c.*, p. 877.

[87] Second Vatican Council, Constitution on the Sacred Liturgy *Sacrosanctum Concilium*, 36 and 63.

pastoral practice.[88] The time has come to evaluate this Commission, its past activity, both the positive and negative aspects, and the guidelines and the help which it has received from the Episcopal Conference regarding its composition and activity. The role of this Commission is much more delicate when the Conference wishes to introduce certain measures of adaptation or inculturation: [89] this is one more reason for making sure that the Commission contains people who are truly competent.

c) The Diocesan Bishop

21. In every diocese the Bishop is the principal dispenser of the mysteries of God, and likewise the governor, promoter and guardian of the entire liturgical life of the Church entrusted to him.[90] When the Bishop celebrates in the midst of his people, it is the very mystery of the Church which is manifested. Therefore it is necessary that the Bishop should be strongly convinced of the importance of such celebrations for the Christian life of his faithful. Such celebrations should be models for the whole diocese.[91] Much still remains to be done to help

[88] Cf. *ibid.*, 44.

[89] Cf. *ibid.*, 40.

[90] Cf. Second Vatican Council, Decree on the Bishops' Office in the Church *Christus Dominus*, 15.

[91] Cf. Address to Italian Bishops attending a course of liturgical renewal (12 February 1988), 1: *L'Osservatore Romano* of 13 February 1988, p. 4.

priests and the faithful to grasp the meaning of the liturgical rites and texts, to develop the dignity and beauty of celebrations and the places where they are held, and to promote, as the Fathers did, a "mystagogic catechesis" of the sacraments. In order to bring this task to a successful conclusion, the Bishop should set up one or more Diocesan Commissions which will help him to promote liturgical activity, music and sacred art in his diocese.[92] The Diocesan Commission, for its part, will act according to the mind and directives of the Bishop and should be able to count upon his authority and his encouragement to carry out its particular task properly.

[92] Cf. Second Vatican Council, Constitution on the Sacred Liturgy *Sacrosanctum Concilium*, 45-46.

CONCLUSION

22. The Liturgy does not exhaust the entire activity of the Church, as the Constitution *Sacrosanctum Concilium* pointed out.[93] It is, however, a source and summit of her activity.[94] It is a source, because, above all from the sacraments, the faithful draw abundantly the water of grace which flows from the side of the Crucified Christ. To use an image dear to Pope John XXIII, it is like the village fountain to which every generation comes to draw water ever living and fresh. It is also a summit, both because all the activity of the Church is directed towards the communion of life with Christ, and because it is in the Liturgy that the Church manifests and communicates to the faithful the work of salvation, accomplished once and for all by Christ.

23. The time has come to renew that spirit which inspired the Church at the moment when the Constitution *Sacrosanctum Concilium* was prepared, discussed, voted upon and promulgated

[93] Cf. *ibid.*, 9.
[94] Cf. *ibid.*, 10.

and when the first steps were taken to apply it. The seed was sown: it has known the rigours of winter, but the seed has sprouted, and become a tree. It is a matter of the organic growth of a tree becoming ever stronger the deeper it sinks its roots into the soil of tradition.[95] I wish to recall what I said at the Congress of Liturgical Commissions in 1984: in the work of liturgical renewal, desired by the Council, it is necessary to keep in mind "with great balance the part of God and the part of man, the hierarchy and the faithful, tradition and progress, the law and adaptation, the individual and the community, silence and choral praise. Thus the Liturgy on earth will fuse with that of heaven, where ... it will form one choir ... to praise with one voice the Father through Jesus Christ".[96]

With this confident hope, which in my heart becomes a prayer, I impart to all my Apostolic Blessing.

Given at the Vatican, on the fourth day of December in the year 1988, the eleventh of my Pontificate.

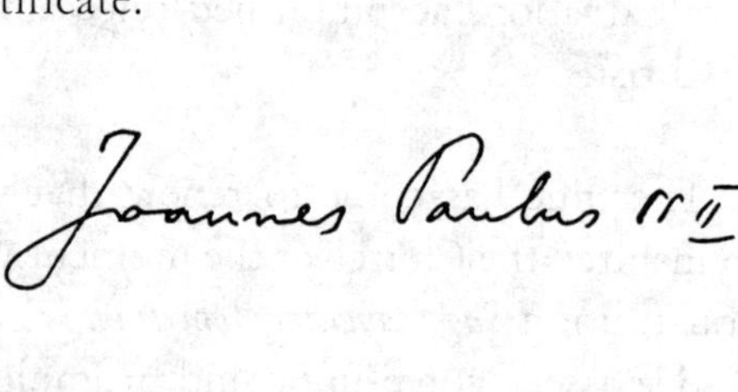

[95] Cf. *ibid.*, 23.

[96] Address to the Congress of Presidents and Secretaries of National Liturgical Commissions (27 October 1984), 6: *Insegnamenti*, VII/2 (1984), p. 1054.

INDEX

The following documents referred to in the text are available from the Catholic Truth Society. Please quote reference numbers when ordering:

Christus Dominus	Do 356
Dei Verbum	Do 361
Dives in Misericordia	Do 526
Dominicae Cenae	Do 519
Familiaris Consortio	S 357
Final Report of 1985 Synod	Do 571
Inter Oecumenici	Do 348
Lumen Gentium	Do 349
Reconciliatio et Paenitentia	Do 562
Redemptor Hominis	Do 506
Sacrosanctum Concilium	Do 386

Further reading also available from CTS:

Study Book for Special Ministers of Holy Communion	3063
The Parish Mass–Bishops' directory	4078
Music in the Parish Mass–Bishops' directory	4450
The Worship of the Eucharist and the Rite of Benediction	4469
A Short History of the Mass–Crichton	5120
The Parish Church–Bishops' directory	566X
Permanent Diaconate–Bishops' directory	7131
Confession–A Practical Approach	D 522
A Simple Penance Book	D 503